sólo tú y yo,
sólo tú y yo, amor mío,
lo escuchamos

—*pablo neruda*

Love, Etc.

poems of love, laughter, longing & loss

l.l. barkat

ts T. S. Poetry Press • New York

T. S. Poetry Press
Ossining, New York
Tspoetry.com

© 2021, 2014 by L.L. Barkat

All rights reserved.

ISBN 978-0-9898542-3-8

Library of Congress Cataloging-in-Publication Data:
Barkat, L.L.
    [Poetry.]
    Love, Etc: Poems of Love, Laughter, Longing & Loss
    ISBN 978-0-9898542-3-8

Library of Congress Control Number: 2014936046

for those who love neruda & poems
—that includes you, maureen—
because I have been meaning to write
a book for you

Contents

Rabia 15
Rabia's Confession 17
Bird on the Mountain 18
Mulberries 21
Winter Road Trip 22
Watching Hero 23
I slept without memory 24
Sometimes 25
After a Poem by David K. Wheeler 26
Lunch at Grand Central 27
Petit à Petit L'Oiseau Fait Son Nid 28
But no 30
You are white smoke against a white sky 31
Combing 32
Embodiment 33
Planted 34
6 a.m. 35
Whispered 36
After Reading Eric Weiner on Iceland 37
Ash Leaves 38
Strategy 39
Un done - Sara Barkat 40
Love Song 42
The Entry 43

Sexy Pie 45
Shoot, girl 47

Roll with me 48
Upon Learning that Fur Was Lost in Translation
(then learning that it wasn't, but too late for this sonnet) .. 49
She: 1341-2011 50
Schedule 51
A man 52
Solo 53
Must-Have Decor 54
I am trying to be 55
Magician 56
Spanish Recipe 57
Proof 58
Meet Me in a Minimalist Poem Where We Can Wear 59
Mixing 60
The Anthologist's Musical Settings 61
I put my finger to my tongue 62
Come to me 63
Crazy Lady 64
Wet 65
Treasures 66
Fantasy 67
Thé 68
Is there such a thing 69
Cook Sugar 70
Mushrooms 71
Laundry love 72
Here's a blush rose 73
Evening Dharani 74
Three Kinds of Pleasures 75
Lay me down 76

Floral 77
Come 78
Field Song 79
You are my golden setting 80
one 81
The dictionary has 82
Punctuation 83
Writing 84

I Love You More 85
Promise 87
I love you more - Sonia Barkat 88
Third Generation, by Phone 89
The Find 90
To the lake, to the ribbon - Sonia Barkat 91
The Words of Your Tattoo You Are Not Going to Get ...92
Morning Prayer 93
one can be 94
Poetry 95
Due to the Loss of Field Roast Artisan Grain Sausage 96
Ours 98
Holding 99
Walk in December 100
The Urging 101
Bringing Forth 102
Pound Ridge, Autumn 103

Etc. 105
Vermillion 107
Envy 108

Après la pluie, le beau temps 109
Purple Bottle Journal 110
Cover 116
After Reading Brad Gooch on Rumi 117
Upon Reading Edward Hirsch, pp. 144-146 118
Neruda's Updated Edition Totals 3,522 Pages 120
Too simple for Ovid 121
Late, I am late 122
Lingual 123
Christmas 124
A Poet's Thanks 125
Maracas 126
Facebook Writer Snacks 127
Choice 128
Poems 129
Leaves stick 130
Sara Teasdale 131

❤

Rabia

Rabia's Confession

You came to me
in marbled echo of men's footsteps,
smoothed leather sandals
removed and placed
at arched doors.

I felt your presence

in ruby silk
they expected me to wear
gold-threaded
unwrapped by hands
that searched for eternity in my breasts.
Jasmine sweat,
skin like cinnamon.

Sometimes when in haste
they lowered themselves too hard, too fast,
Your voice startled in the small shatter
of a glass bangle
that fell from my wrist

clink, clink, clink

taking with it
the tiniest offering
of blood.

Bird on the Mountain

1

If you write without ceasing,
you will find fragments of Psalms
on the body, in the hair,
in the brown eyes
imprinted with desire lines.
The lines will take you where you want to go
on the body, in the hair,
in the brown eyes
that blink like beaded pearls,
bird-eye pearls
strung along the body
of a hair-tangled
mountain.

2

I built my desire lines
across your body—
shoulder to tip of thumb,
neck bone
to cupped cream-soft spine,
hip rise
to hip rise

3

If you would lower
your standards,
eat fragments of Psalms,
not require the aperitif,
the blackberry on the ridge
of a pastry,
pork pulled in trails
across plates.
If you could
be content with knowing
that an empty glass
is an invitation,
you could stop refusing
your fortune.

4

Don't flee from me any longer,
small bird with the brown
flecked wings—
I have held out my hands
on this mountain
for so long
that my desire lines
are planted deep across
the rise of my palms.

5

The *to* is
anticipation,
like the bird flying
to
her mountain,
like the brown eyes
looking
to
open the trails
scattered
with fallen trees,
like the mountain's
thousand-year journey
to the sea.

6

When does the bird
begin to flee
to her mountain?
When does she make
the plan,
pack nothing
for the journey
but a piece of straw
she has not yet
found.

Mulberries

1

While the mourning dove
is still sleeping,
before the sun can waken her,
I kneel beneath the mulberry tree.
You will know this without me speaking
when you open my stained palm.

2

Will you.

3

Long now,
I have missed the mulberries.

Winter Road Trip

The road is long as I travel south
and the sun is low in the white sky.
Last night I woke to a great silence,
in a house that is anything but silent
by day. Old pines keep watch
over that dwelling, and the moon
keeps watch, and I wish
for this kind of watching,
but my bedroom in the town where I live
looks out over streetlights and the sounds
of cars and sometimes sirens. In my room,
the roads seem short, and I wonder
if tonight I will dream of the long road
home, and how the sun bathed the trees
in gold, and how the sumacs leaned with flowers
the color of some wine whose name
I can't remember, near the trees whose names
I've never known, now strung with long red necklaces.

Watching Hero

The sheet was red
and silken.

It lay between us,
and the man
and the woman
he took to bed.

Some things,
says Young,
must be made
opaque
to be seen.

I am still
satisfied
that I showed
the screen
to my children;
hidden elbows, knees,
pointing the way
to intimate
distress.

I slept without memory,
woke, yes. Always waking

but slept again
without memory.

Rose.
In the morning

Neruda said the same.
I was a rose, *diminuta y desnuda*.

Sometimes,
when I'm alone,
I put the tip of the sheet
into my mouth. It's this primal
thing, this pressing of the edge
into my very self.

After a Poem by David K. Wheeler

The silence goes further back.
I thought of that today. It was the way
we were told to be seen and not heard,
and pinched if we transgressed at the table.
It was the way he slept in the living room by night
and looked through us by day, as if we didn't exist,
as if we made   no sound   at all.

Lunch at Grand Central

She saw it happen,
she explained.
The heart, all hooked up.
He nodded as she gestured
to her chest. *The lungs are here,*
she said. *And the heart is behind them.*
Yes, he seemed to know
all about it. *They do heart surgery
through the back*, he said.
She did not deny it, just went on
speaking of the heart's troubles,
never stopping to consider
the actual point of entry.

Petit à Petit L'Oiseau Fait Son Nid

Little by little, they say,
the bird makes its nest.
I have been making mine
in silvered hemlocks, time
after time; today I used a red
thread I found near the garden.

I used to dream of living in a garden,
listening to words white orchids say
to emerald hummingbirds, red-
throated, stealing gold for nests
the size of women's thimbles, time
beating between breaths, a rhythm mine

could never find trapped, as in a mine
long hollowed, tapped black garden
that metamorphosed over time,
caught sounds of earth-on-earth say,
Come bed yourself on rock-hard nest,
turn death to sapphire, diamond, ruby red.

Rumor spreads: inside the earth is red,
molten, thrusting gold like mine
into the sun, into evening's nest
that sits above an empty garden
where orchids do not say
it is time

it is time
to ravel rays from ravished dreams, red
and unremembered; it is time to say
what is yours and what is mine
it is time to turn the garden
into earth, find fool's gold for a nest.

I have been making such a nest,
little by little, time after time,
I have been dreaming near a garden
in threads of memories, ruby red.
I have been claiming what is mine
and inviting you to say

you want the nest, the gold turning red,
the time we knew was mine,
the garden waiting, for what you have to say.

But no,

maybe she would say
something altogether different.

Something like—
he cannot remember the verb
for me,
nor the breath to make the sentences.
The glass never tips,
the incomprehensible music does not
play,
the voice, the door, the rain (the rain?),
even the rain, especially the rain,
and the sheer cotton blouse, wet,
we no longer see.

You are white smoke against a white sky.
I can barely see you drifting by my window
on this morning of white sheets against white skin.
I can barely feel your breath, thin as it is over the maples
fusing orange to yellow to orange to red.

I open the glass.

To let me out, to let you in.

Combing

We walk along the deserted beach,
leaning to touch shells—
their ridged backs telling us
a story, the words of which
we cannot hear, only feel.

Sometimes

we take them home, thinking
we will find a place for them
on the window sill,
but the light isn't quite right
and the garden has a little spot
where the pink begonias grow in Spring
that simply seems

wanting

Does it matter now?

Why we brought them home,
why the sill was not
where we eventually laid them
to a curved white rest.

Embodiment

No one thinks of it
this way,

thinks about incarnation

being

what we do
when we say *this is the truth*

of what I am living
day to day

and it hurts like hell
to be the ones

to put it
into body,

but we cannot
seem to help ourselves.

The truth
is being born
under our fingertips.

Planted

It was supposed to be
a dogwood, I thought—
flowering.
So I planted the tree
in the middle
of my little rock garden,
the one with the broken white shells,
the one where rosemary
sometimes overwinters
sometimes dies
into a stiff thrush
of ruined pungency.
How many years now?
The tree still
not in bloom.
I prune her height
back to the center,
where today she is ringed
with red begonias,
strung with morning's circle
of empty sunlight.

6 a.m.

You know the echo
of nothing.
How the bed beside you
is empty
and the sheets seem
extra loud
against themselves.
The sun has barely risen
and a light breeze
has picked up
after the lonely night.
You cannot feel the air moving,
but the sound of the shade
keeps knocking
its hollow knuckle
at the old wooden sill.

Whispered

I should tell you
about my hands, small
and experienced.

The other night,
when my youngest daughter
said, as I tucked her into bed,

Tell me something. Tell me anything,
I turned off the light and whispered this:

when I cut the beets tonight,
the red water went all into
the lines on my hands—

so many lines.

After Reading Eric Weiner on Iceland

This pondering darkness
I understand, this
groping the sky
you know is blue
somewhere, this
search for the switch
to illumine the moon.
It must be there;
you saw it once
hanging over
Manhattan.

Ash Leaves

Near the corner of the drive,
brown ridged dried spears
of Ash or an unnamed swamp tree
hug each other's tips and stems—
their backs paralyzed in ice
their rustlings gone silent.

Strategy

My business plan
was to meet women,
which I accomplished.
I wish I could remember
their names.

Un done

The end of the day does not break, like glass—
maybe; you can catch it, with broken string
on an old piano, *black notes white notes*
falling out the window and the shatter—
bends. Breaks. The other cacophony sits
silently watching, fingers bend like wood

looks on the bench; here the wind through the wood
like broken wind chimes—in a pile of glass—
swallows, noiselessly, the sunrise; and sits.
The whistle doesn't know the sound of string
softly shushing sound asleep, but shatters
silence with faint white *almost-music-notes*

climbing up the wall and through the roof, notes—
sing in a voice like ivory and wood
higher and higher above the shatters
of your glass, *tall slim clear glass*
and at the very top; tips, trips, *falls…* strings
descending, rushing, howling, and—sits.

Upon the ground, other melodies sit
writes out letters in a shaky hand, notes
in brown ink; one by one pulls up the strings
wrestles with song, a savage battle, wood
stained with inky blood—or bloody ink—glass
overturned; lying in pieces, shatters.

And… silence. …Darkness. *Don't look—it shatters
if you look at it too hard* but… here, sits
under the sky; plucking stars, shining glass,
sewing them into a cloak—bejeweled notes
like the firmament itself; they all would
hang like gossamer, silver spider strings.

Test it out for yourself. Wrapped tight with strings,
you strain to pull free; frenzied, soft, shatters
to lie flung across the old stone, old wood
whispers in your ear; tells you, *sit, sit, sit*—
listen to the voice in the wind, the notes
in the old piano, encased in glass.

Carve out a tree from wood, it falls in strings—
push the glass out a window, it shatters—
and when you're tired, sit—hear the last notes.

Sara Barkat, age 15

Love Song

My table is long,
my window open.

Are you a ghost?

        Come anyway.

I have saved you

a yellow pear
and a small knife.

You will say,
what is a pear
to a ghost?
What is a knife?

I will say, let's sit together
in the morning.

You shall peel the pear.
I shall hold my hands

beneath your white,
under the knife,

and catch for us
        the long sun spirals.

The Entry

It is a slow arousal—
the rain, and how it moves

across the earth still sleeping.

How it reaches rivulets
into myriad cracks, holes,
gaps that winter forced.

The rain slides in, everywhere,
swelling, and the earth
awakes, absorbs and rejoins

itself to itself.

♥

Sexy Pie

Shoot, girl,
where the hell
did you get all these poems?
Have you been hiding them
in your attic,
down your shirt,
beneath your tongue
below your pout?

Hasn't it been hard
to keep them all in
everywhere they've been
flinging off their underthings,
trying to get out?

Roll with me,

let's see.

**Upon Learning that Fur Was Lost in Translation
(then learning that it wasn't, but too late for this sonnet)**

What did fine French Cinder *elles* wear besides
glass, what high class did they hope to flaunt to
the ball, what gall muster towards, *I do*?
Did they eat ash, secret, pretend inside,
ache for privileges to take midnight steed ride—
to prince, to price, to prove flamed thoughts, undo
braided tresses, guesses; did they have clues
about the way ever-after collides

in fives, in tens, muttered end lines tight shut,
a fight to rise between odd hours ticking,
tripping like a *da-dum* tapped short, slight cut
into small rooms, *I am's* that jam, turning
coated slippers towards spondee minutes
spent as splintered moments on silk shorn string?

She: 1341-2011

I am the curved mistress of poetry's
men who open their lips with words of wine
to niggle pearl buttons, white spines soft-tease
tongued vertebra, linked like a compline

sweet-whispered with slight syllables: *Laura*.
Laura worn on the mouth, laid on the head,
not of a long-dead Petrarchan *sola*,
leaved with twined curled vines, climbing feathered bed

peeking near edges sheeting trills: *mi, mi, mi*,
rolling out rhyme for Valentine pledges,
proving Hamlet's hope to be or not be
remembered, ravished, rent from dark ledges.

I am the fire you could never let kiss
you. *Laura*, salt-taste of unquenched bright bliss.

Schedule

I wanted to end
the week with you.
Then I wondered,
why not begin the night
with you,
and would it be so terrible
if I carried it over
to breakfast
and a cup of something
hot to drink
with you?

A man
can be a cup,
if he sits very still
and loves repetition.

Solo

Living alone has got its effects—
like, for instance, one goes without...
well, if one chose one could

but one needn't. In any case,
take tonight in the bath, where
dishes I did. Which is not the same,

by the way, as me being unlaced
doing scrub a dub dub in a tub
with the plates. No, my sink

in the kitchen is clogged. So I
barely got wet, just my hands,
caressing the forks and the pans.

Must-Have Decor

I do not know the names
of enough flowers. I love them
all, but I cannot place their tongues,
their petals in a nomenclature
fit to hold their fragrances.
Today, however,
I know there is a white orchid
on my kitchen counter,
near the white stove.
Maybe this will make you laugh,
but I looked at that flower
this morning and thought
it looked like sex,
and I mused that I should
keep one always, right here
on the counter.

I am trying to be
sensibly derailed
      by you

and your

      w
ords

Falling off the hours,
the way you make
me (take me)

is

so

gratifying

I

      am dashing my days

into little pieces

of
      panting

l   ov   e

Magician

You should see me
here at the stove,
shaking things
into the soup pot,
flicking salt and pepper
like fairy dust
over the bubbles rising,
stirring spirals
that could hypnotize
the skimpiest eater
into spooning love.

Spanish Recipe

1

Let's make
Neruda soup together.
You bring the poems,
I'll bring the red poppies
and the black seeds.

2

Let's eat
the soup together.
You bring an open mouth,
I'll bring a full spoon.

Proof

I wanted to prove I could write
a different kind of poem, so I looked
around the kitchen for a likely subject.

Do you have any idea how uncooperative
a kitchen can be, especially at dinner time.
Really. Red pears, bleeding clear juice. The chili
burning my lips with both its heat and spice.
A green bottle of tonic water on the counter,
its fizz spent. Notes to myself, everywhere,
such a simple yet intimate thing.

I can't even tell you about the laundry,
half-folded, half strewn, touched by my fingers
which so lately peeled the onions
down to their skins. And now I'm at the chili
again, stirring and stirring,
proving how resistant to objectivity
a kitchen can be.

Meet Me in a Minimalist Poem Where We Can Wear

(   )

Mixing

```
d
    d
e
        e
    s
i
        i
    r


  e
```

The Anthologist's Musical Settings

So I bought this book
of Elizabethan verse, songs,
you know, with actual musical settings.
And I was so glad to have that—
couches backed and arched with silk,
brocade, curtains pulled just right to permit
only the bare minimum of light to fall
upon a woman's arm. Pianos with ivory keys
(the real kind, see). God, and all those legs
under the weight of all those crimson vases.
There were so many golden things, waiting
to be traced beneath my searching fingers.
And, oh! The lace, the laces.

I put my finger to my tongue,
let it warm, let it wet.
I put my finger to you
and stir, and stir.

Come to me,
my skin is velvet.
The night a veil.
The kiss, a meting out
of ebony, a rising of
the transparent
                      tip.

Crazy Lady

Blues, she wears
blues. Denim.
Or cotton black.
Skin, she wears
skin. Yours. Hers.
You, she wears
you. On her crazy
thoughts, on her
long black hair.
She wears. Your
blues.

Wet

Have you.
I mean, not by accident
in some unwelcome downpour.
Have you let the rain
come down, over your hair
your cheeks
your lips.
Have you let it blur
your sight?

On the other side
stands a girl
in white,
and the rain
is finding her secret places,
making them visible to you
when you blink
your eyes.

Treasures

I put my fingers
to your face. There, ivory.
I put my belly to your belly.
There, rubies.
To your mouth, I put
my mouth. Pearl, and more
pearl. I put my toes between
your knees, and trace upwards.
Jewels, jewels!

Fantasy

If I had endless money,
I would spend it endless with you.
On caramel drinks, and days by the sea,
walking over white sand and pink shells.
I would open my body beneath the moon,
my arm finding your waist, my fingers
playing near the hollow that remembers
your birth. I would unbind our burdens
(would we have any?), and untie our tongues,
with cocktails and floating orchids.
We would read (and I would write)
poetry, and sleep, yes sleep,
before and after love.

Thé

It's a terrible name
for a tea, but I can't help myself:
Thé des Concubines.
If I told you what was in it,
you'd think: too much cherry, mango,
vanilla can't be good.
If I told you I put my finger
across the saucer
while I tipped the cup,
would you want to know about
the little lip in the center, and how my skin
suddenly felt all cherry-mango-vanilla?

Is there such a thing
as disposable sexy pie?
Does it come in aluminum, flimsy?

Cook Sugar

Instructions
           for making
candy:

One thick-bottomed pot
(hot).

One flame,
           turned on
low.

Sugar.
So much *sugarsugarsugarsugar*.

A hand
    to stir.

and
      stir
and
        stir.

One tongue
    to lick
the spoon (wait 'til
        cool).

Mmmm.

Mushrooms

Just you and I,
let's truffle
let's shiitake
let's button (and unbutton).

Laundry love
is tangled shirts
the hem of a skirt
caught
in the brass button
of your jeans.

Here's a blush rose,
with raspberry scent.

Here's a pink,
come taste the edge.

And here, my dear,
upon the stair,
is simply the hip
of a white-blue rose
I've carried up
to bed.

Evening Dharani

Comma, comma, comma, comma
come a, come a, come a, come a,
cum a, cum a, cum a, cum a
cama, cama, cama, cama.

Three Kinds of Pleasures

You, in the morning.

In the afternoon, you.

Evening, of course   you   you   you.

Lay me down
beneath the oak.
Let us leave tracks
in the last of autumn.
Run your hand
over the miles.

Floral

Tucked tongue, *o, u, o, u, o, u,*
cultivates purple buttercupped
begonias. Where hibiscus, oh hibiscus,
blooms and blooms and blooms.

Come,
dip your little finger   in

Field Song

And my fingers,
stirring seed
into the furrows.

You are my golden setting,
all my amethysts are yours
held firm in the rim of you.

one
little
button
at a
time

The dictionary has
so many delicious words
in and around
the page that contains
suggestions.

Punctuation

*When the woman is on her back
and the man lies on top of her
it is the cedilla.*

— Breton, from "Mad Love"

And before that
the question   mark

Writing

I stand by the mirror,
letting down my hair, strand
by brown cherry strand.

You stand by the door,
leaning.

I slip off a white silk
robe, lined with shadow.

You are as one, in an orchard.

And when I turn
to reach for another word,
and the small curve of my flesh
moves into light,

you take the nippled blossoms
onto your tongue.

♥

I Love You More

Promise

A mountain, as the mist descends,
is a promise. We must trust
that its age-old myths
are still alive in the grey birches,
in the birches white, black and silver
stripped. We must lace our bodices
and sing to the livening air, understanding
that the deep knowledge of earth's roots
still thrusts itself into woodbine,
sorrel, bulbous mushrooms (orange),
where the fairies place their little beds,
and beckon you to pleats and folds
of little see-through tents.

I love you more
than flowers

and seven tall towers

For you
I have powers
of love.

Sonia Barkat, age 7

Third Generation, by Phone

At times she stops
listening to you,
because all she wants to hear
is your voice.

The Find

To me it is just
a cave—a bouldered space
held dark against this mountain.
To you, it opens
dreams of dragons, pink and green
as the dragon-scale shoes
I bought for you just yesterday,
knowing it would be too soon before
you came upon this place, only to find it had become
just a cave, an empty bouldered space.

To the lake, to the ribbon
red, to the time of Kantay,
to the purple shell to the
day of Portlant to the year
of 280 to the place you know
to the people you love, to the
things you think to the places
you dream of, to the light you
seek to what keeps you from
wondering to the love you
give to the love you receive
to what you know is the secret
to the path that you know
is the road to follow.

Sonia Barkat, age 9

The Words of Your Tattoo You Are Not Going to Get

Podemos,
juntos
podemos.

Morning Prayer

This is the day,
let it be the day of the poem
today, today, today

for my loves
who I care for
and who You care for
more than I ever could

because, of course,
You are God.

one can be

a door

        a handle

a
     t
   u
   r
    n
        ing

all part of
                opening

Poetry

Poems say too much,
or they know too little.

Poems are how I found you,
and how I lost you.

Every day I think,
I should stop writing poems.

Due to the Loss of Field Roast Artisan Grain Sausage

Under the pastry board
that pulls out like an awning,
I found her. Half in, half out
of a cabinet door,
its shelter a hard cloak
that could hide the tears.

She was weeping
because we forgot to leave her
more than one ring
of spicy sausage.

Come here,

I told her, and gathered her
thirteen-year-old frame
into my arms, pulled her
towards my warm body.

I love that you are crying about sausage,

I said. And she rolled her eyes
like I was just some crazy mama
trying to comfort with nonsense.

No, really,

I whispered. Because, I told her,
not everyone would cry about sausage.
She might be a famous chef someday
or a travel and food writer.

Such a person might cry
under an awning in New York
or Paris, about a sausage,
or a lost link to some recipe
from the past.

Ours

We call them to the world
before we even know their names,
before we understand
what it will mean
to lean beside their beds
on breath-thin nights.

They teach us
how to hold their hands,
shut the lights,
pray for dawn.

Holding

Put on your blue boots
better in the snow
let's go watch
the glow of the Hungry Moon

forge a memory
like the one my mother
gave to me at two in the morning
rousing from comfort of sheets and dreams
to see the Northern Lights shimmering
green pink blue—inverted funnel I fell into,
upward towards this future
I did not know was mine, under
the pine holding hands
with my two girls
beneath the Hungry Moon.

Walk in December

This is jewel-tree corner
where I held your hand
and the streetlights
looked on, and I wanted
to keep the moment
beyond what seemed possible
permissible

keep

the pressure of your fingers
against mine
and the ice clinging
to bare branches

sparkling
like pink Depression glass.

The Urging

I sent my girls
into the cold rain.
Go, I told them,
ignoring how
they hung back
by the door.
I pointed
to the red maple,
noted
that it was strung
with a crystal necklace.

They were gone
for hours,

making rain-secrets.

Bringing Forth

On the gold rock,
we used to sit
with our primitive poles.
Sticks we gathered
from grandmother's
broken maples,
pins we tied by the head
onto white string.
The sunnies swam
brown-golden-rainbow
in her lake, near the sand beach
she brought in
herself. We always cheered
when we hooked
the surge of body and fin.
But I also cried
at the blood, the shining hole,
and more often than not
I threw the breathless sunnies
back in.

Pound Ridge, Autumn

There are so many years
between us,
like these fields
now stand between us; you never stop
moving South, touching
tops of bronzed grass bending
to the weight of September.
I hold quite still, note
that you don't look back.
And I don't want
to look forward.

♥

Etc.

Vermillion

The words in my house
were flat,
one syllable,
hard beginnings
or endings,
easy to line up–
like wooden dominoes–
easy to use, remember.

I spent years

trying to replace them
with a fluency of crimson
indigo emerald lapis
vermillion (how I loved
vermilion when I found it).

And still I haunt

Neruda Akhmatova
Darwish's girl, her spirit
transparent as apricots in March,
looking for—what?

Something rounder
than what I was given,
something beyond black and white,
something like blown red glass.

Envy

I am jealous of the red flower,
I'll admit it. Poets can be that way,
wanting to be the one
who the gods choose to visit in a rush,
wanting to be the one
whose neck is grasped
with the first flush
of whatever it might be:
the numinous petal, the sensual dew,
the feather (oh yes, the white feather).

Après la pluie,
le beau temps

After the rain,
après la pluie. After.

Après the weight of grey,
words that stray, slant,
sending swallows
(*hirondelles*)

to hemlock arms—sway,
spring, sway. After
the rain, *après*.

Le beau temps come.

Good weather hurries in,
on the heels of wind. So
they say.

Purple Bottle Journal

1

Where does a poem begin?
Where does the life of a poet begin?
Paul Chowder says to begin a poem anywhere.
That is a likely enough place.
We can begin right here with the purple bottles
and then we can go anywhere.

2

This is eternity right in our brains.
There is no beginning or end.
No timeline we must walk along for miles
before getting where we want to go.
The brain is fractal. The brain branches.
It is a river to the sea and rain from the sky
and a mist rising back to the clouds
all in fractal radiance and we can touch down,
touch in, touch up anywhere.
There is no alpha and omega,
although the alpha and omega
is stored inside a string of *a-b-c*'s.
But even these are not strictly strung,
a having come from our grandmother in 1966
and *b* having come from our mother
when she blew kisses to us near the window
and *f* has its comforts and its terrors—

having both our father's love of fire
(and how he would tend one for hours
and watch the ephemeral-eternal flames),
but f is also our step-father
ranting about our f—ing nigger-bastard asses
sitting on his clean chairs around his f—ing table
(and you just now wonder about all the possibilities
of an f—king table, and so f has become that too for you).
You see both the finite and infinite possibilities of your brain.

3

Paul Chowder says
it does not matter if a poem is true.
He doesn't care.
And Tim O'Brien says the true war story
is the one you feel in your gut.

       So the boy's face
              slid off
                      in one story version,
and in another version the grenade
        was caught
        by the boy
        first. (BOOM!)

But I am probably remembering that wrong.

Somewhere I read an article that said
we sometimes remember poetry wrong
because, after all, that is the rightest way.

In Tim O'Brien's war story, a boy walks onto the front
with his girl's pantyhose tight around his neck,
perhaps the way he remembered her legs around his hips.
Is it true? Of course it is true. Just like the man in Young's book,
who said the war bodies were wax.

Insanity and sanity both have their truths,
and sometimes they are inextricable.
What I love about a poem?
I can be sane or insane and it doesn't matter.

You get my purple truth.

4

Who writes letters this long,
to a perfect stranger?

She wrote to me,
asking all manner of questions
including, could I tell her how a poet
finds new metaphors. As if I could

pull out my how-to-be-a-poet notes
and craft a timely response.

How do you find the new?
How does a poet go about being a poet?

You go to the ravine where your sister
used her bare feet as skis, careened
down the bronze pine needles,
and where she dug with her bare hands
and found broken china, blue and white,
like it was from Holland,
like Holland had visited the white pines
and watched you escape for another day,
from the cigarettes and fingernails with tar
from their tips to their moons. Had Holland
looked on when your mother took a knife
and screamed that she would cut his heart out?
What did the yellow tulips think of a woman
who would do that to save your sister
(her tiny neck turning red from his grip)?

Out in the woods, where the pines thinned
to the down-curve where she careened,
your sister found the bottles too.
They may have been blue,
you tell the woman
who wrote you the too-long letter.

But you want to remember them purple.

5

I want to ask the woman,
when was the last time
you went searching
for a metaphor?

All metaphor first existed
in the landscape. Somebody
said that somewhere;
maybe it was Edward Hirsch.
Or Kim Addonizio.
I lose track of who has told me what,
about poetry and language.

So I want to tell the woman,
go, the way I went today
and a red bird flushed
from the red canes
as I rounded the curve
of the horse trail.
The canes were stripped,
and maybe you will see
a woman in them, or your
very soul, and you will wish
you were a stripper,
no longer holding out
on the world, but rather
bending your back
to the afternoon light,

your spine-buds
like the pricking points
of the wine berries' naked limbs,
their whole bodies leafless
for the winter to come.
There you might find
your metaphor.

6

And so the truth is
that as much as we love to be alone,
we want to be together.
It is the paradox of the poem,
playing out in our very life.
The poem is most usually written in solitude.
The poem is a lonely thing,
as we are a lonely thing.
Yet the poem is unabashedly purple
(let the Reader curse and condemn if he wants to!
He shall have to take on Neruda and Whitman,
Hafiz and Akhmatova too,
and that is a formidable cursing
should one wish to undertake it).

Cover

And it is one of those mornings
where anything can make me cry.
The tangerine book cover with painted cloves,
nutmeg (whole), a small cup
of sour cherries (so red like glass)
and the figs sliced open
to their pink centers, little seeds
all glistening.

After Reading Brad Gooch on Rumi

He made a peach
famous, first because
he ate it. Then because
he wrote it.

Upon Reading Edward Hirsch, pp. 144-146

Poems are presences,
he says, and I am struck
by the soul
I see today, though I have been
to these pages
in the past.

Wallace is here, whispering,
This is the intensest rendezvous.
And Bogan, *Now that I have your heart*
by heart,
I see.

Basho is speaking of a windswept spirit
which he has made it his business
to capture in poems. He tells his secret
in November, a few days before his death,
which startles me
with its resemblance
to my birth day.
He speaks of final
wandering dreams and withered fields.
His poem a presence now, a meeting
with Wallace and Louise
and me, walking our own fields
for a time, feeling our own wind
on our own skin. I have picked
a bouquet of black-eyed-susans,

the flower that reminds my mother
of brown-eyed me.
I am holding them out, heart beating
rendezvous, rendez vous.

Neruda's Updated Edition Totals 3,522 Pages

It is no secret, they say,
that his work is unbalanced.
How could it be
otherwise
given his astonishing output?

Man of dark poppies.
Man of amor
and war.
Solitary, yet written bodied, bodied
into the minds
of the people.

It is no secret (to me)
that each day
I hand you yet another page
of my own dark poppy heart
unbalanced
of course, because it simply
keeps beating (for better or worse)

words, words, words, words, words.

Too simple for Ovid
and Homer,
I rinse these words
with nothing
but bare hands.

Late, I am late.
And Homer is moving down the centuries
without my story.

Lingual

Sometimes I wonder
about the origin
of words. This one,
for instance: *palpable*.
Can you feel it?
Did someone wake up
one morning and find
it had appeared on his tongue,
an errant (but perfect)
leftover from a dream?

Christmas

I learned patience
on the floor.
I can still feel the lines
of our linoleum
under my fingers
as I crawled and stifled
my breathing,
listening to his breathing
heavy with smoke
and the day's curses
sloughing off
into night, into the unliving
living room.
Snow outside,
ice within, pristine
as the waterfall
now paralyzed out back.
On the paneled wall,
near the windowed door
hung a plush red stocking
filled by my mother's hand.
I crawled for hours,
it seemed, to reach
that velvet candy cane.

A Poet's Thanks

Off in another city, or maybe a clean quiet town
with brick homes and front yards of rhododendrons,
bloomless azaleas, you are doing something today.
Are you a cook? Is it you who's involved in peeling,
slicing, stuffing, baking? Or maybe you are with a book,
or a child is playing at your feet.

I am here, playing with words, my heart filled with something
you could call thankfulness, but which is much wider than that.
Something which says, you didn't need to make room for
    this—
the onions, the beets, the linen closet, the river and the copper
Palisades. Your life was full without my words, but you've
    held me
in a space out back, near the red tree, and I am like a flute
set amidst the leaves, singing when the wind moves through.

Maracas

no fingers,
no sound

Facebook Writer Snacks

Your favorite snack?
I asked the writers.

They told me
the muse feeds them
green olives, pan-fired tea,
tears splashed
on strawberries filled
with creamy cheesecake.

For the desperate,
she holds a metal can
of spray *fromage*
right into their mouths,
squeezing a plastic nipple
onto their raised buds.

The guilty repent
with requests for edamame
and apple wedges.

The lush word lovers
can't stop drinking
espresso and beer.

Choice

When a man has been touching poems
for a long time,
counting lines, putting his fingers on spaces
as if they were the urgent holes
of a Red Lancewood flute,
he begins to wonder what makes him remember.

(His desirous palm must have its reasons.)

Is it the way a veil slipped off a body (hers),
or a certain catch of breath (his),
or perhaps the way he kept the page open
with the head of a brass elephant—its many arms
and bells, like fringes, summoning a god.

What imprints itself without permission on the mind,
makes the almond amygdala surrender
as if to a hot kiss of clove and cinnamon?

What stains? (Surely not the chioggias, which are too light,
too peppermint-candy striped.)

What makes him return, as to his own body,
bright and open on a bed? Is it the simple presence
of a searching tongue—hers/his?

Poems

I love them, you know.
All your little beaded words.
The tiger-eyed ones, the Italian
red glass (with the foil inside).
I love the way you line them up,
as on a golden thread. The onyx,
the abalone, even the dark brown
wood ones all carved and oblong.
I keep them in a velvet-throated box,
and when I am alone, I put my fingers
all through their crystal chattering.

Leaves stick
to my black wool gloves.
Sun shines
on my winter face.
I shake last year's residue
into the wheel barrow.

Sara Teasdale

I like the way Paul Chowder
speaks so lovingly
of Sara Teasdale, and how
he forgives her for her dirty limericks,
even wishes she hadn't burned them.
He knows she kept on with Vachel
even so, even though they never married.
Because Sara loved Vachel, and maybe he loved
her limericks, and, my God, don't we need
somebody to love the side of us
we are always burning for fear?

Also from T. S. Poetry Press

Rumors of Water: Thoughts on Creativity & Writing, by L.L. Barkat (Twice named a Best Book of 2011)

A few brave writers pull back the curtain to show us their creative process. Annie Dillard did this. So did Hemingway. Now L.L. Barkat has given us a thoroughly modern analysis of writing. Practical, yes, but also a gentle uncovering of the art of being a writer.

— Gordon Atkinson, Editor at Laity Lodge

The Novelist: A Novella, by L.L. Barkat

To state the pleasurable, Barkat is a damn fine writer. Her prose is elegant without becoming stuffy, plus the poetry included within the text is astonishing in its range and individuality of styles. Truly, this is the kind of *tour* from which springs *de force*.

—Hubert O'Hearn, former editor *Herald de Paris* and Contributing Editor *San Francisco Book Review*

T. S. Poetry Press titles are available online in e-book and print editions. Print editions also available through Ingram.

tspoetry.com

www.ingramcontent.com/pod-product-compliance
Lightning Source LLC
Chambersburg PA
CBHW022118040426
42450CB00006B/757